Sp7t

Animals

By KIDSLABEL

chronicle books · san francisco

The pairs of photos in this book of picture riddles seem the same...

but look carefully.
There are 7 differences.

You'll also find a **riddle** below each pair of photos.
Need a clue? The answer is always something
in the pictures above.

Extra Challenge
Looking only at the right-hand pages (and don't forget
the front cover!), find:

18 **butterflies**
9 **giraffes**
2 **ladybugs**
2 **basketballs**
1 **green balloon**

and an apple.

He clasps the crumbs with little hands;
close to the ground in giants' lands,
before the baited trap he stands.

Behind the baseboard's edge he peeks;
along the kitchen floor he sneaks,
over the feet he finds there . . . *Eek!*

Peanut butter and jelly; pickle relish and ham;
lettuce and tomato; potato chips and jam.
Whatever type of sandwich is your favorite, you'll agree
that whatever you put in it, it's not a sandwich without me.

People think I'm silly,
but I couldn't tell you why—
how many things can *you* name
that can walk, and swim, and fly?

Here are two picture riddles, also called *rebuses.*

1.    + ⟋ − fin

2.   ⬭ + ⤬ − rt

Hook the sound of *gh* in *laughter*,
net the *o* in *women*, and after,
catch from *nation* both *t* and *i*.
Say them together. What's the thing,
in any weather, that never can stay dry?

Ooo, I feel a little sick.
Maybe I had too many rocks for lunch?
I hate to be abrupt,
but I'm feeling kind of shaky. Is it hot in here?
I think I might . . .

FOR SALE, slightly used. Leather(y) upholstery. Roomy trunk.
For the rider who prefers style to speed. Sorry, no keys.

This wanderer takes his time to get there.
On his road he's always alone.
But he's so cleverly dressed
that when he's at rest
he's home.

What is it
can hold a well of water,
makes buckets lighter,
can be dug down,
but not dug up?

If you are hungry drop me.
Another will snap me up.
Then we two will come home with you,
but only you will sup.

yellow   skin,
soft within.   yellow skin,
soft within. yellow skin, soft within. yellow
skin, soft within. yellow skin, soft within. yellow skin, soft within.

Let's play
a counting game:
You hold me in your hands
and I will try to trip your feet.
For how many turns can you keep the beat?

Front and Back Covers: Look for
an animal at the top near a blue marble
an elephant in a corner
a lion on the 7
a rock on the 7
an animal at the top left
a hippo near a green cylinder
an animal near a white marble

Animals on Board: Look for
an animal game piece at the top of the
  game board
a duck on the right
a green pebble on the game board
an animal game piece near the game
  board's bottom left corner
a green stone at the bottom of the
  picture
a spot on a cow
a crack in a pale square

Around Town: Look for
an animal in the middle of the street
a ball on the left
a poster on a wall
a cat by a trash can
a gray cat with an orange cat
a clock
a brick above a café sign

On the Farm: Look for
the trail behind an airplane
a balloon by a fluffy elephant
a butterfly above a barn
a pig behind a tree
a cow in the middle
a horse behind a tree
a giraffe

In the Bamboo Jungle: Look for
a dragon at the top left
a tiger climbing down the bamboo
another tiger climbing up
a panda near the top
a tear-shaped jewel
a panda near a pheasant
a lion

An Ice Day: Look for
a penguin looking at a whale
a penguin on the left
a penguin on the right
a penguin behind two others who are
  looking at each other
a penguin with a bow tie
a penguin by a seal
a fish

March of the Dinosaurs: Look for
a pterodactyl
a camel
a volcano
an elephant
a yellow dinosaur near the bottom
a green dinosaur on the right
a dinosaur with a crest near the bottom

Block City: Look for
a sign at the top right
an elephant near a dog
a spaceship near a parking sign
a ladybug
a teddy bear
a number 2
an excavator

In the Garden: Look for
a leaf at the top left
a beetle
an ant on a piece of wood
a grasshopper on a leaf
a pinecone by a stick
a rose by a sunflower
a butterfly at the bottom left

Underground: Look for
a red candy
a mole
an ant between two leaves
some pink flowers
something near five stars
a cracker
an ant at the top right

Frog Holiday: Look for
a fish hook
a frog on a rock
a pearl ring
a plant behind a rock
a tadpole
a pebble at the bottom left
an artistic frog

What a Doll: Look for
a penguin at the top left
a banana
a little elephant
a pig
a hedgehog
a rhino
a cat on the right

Toy Corner: Look for
a lion on the wall
a little duck on top of a big one
a cork in a bottle
a dog hanging out on the right
a little teddy bear on a rocker
a turtle
a rooster on the carpet

Answers to the riddles:
Animals on Board: mouse
Around Town: bread
On the Farm: duck
In the Bamboo Jungle: tiger, panda
An Ice Day: fish
March of the Dinosaurs: volcano
Block City: elephant
In the Garden: snail
Underground: hole
Frog Holiday: hook
What a Doll: banana
Toy Corner: jump rope
(Jumping rope is a counting game, and
so is this poem: if you count, the
syllables in each line go 2-4-6-8-10)

Still can't find them?
Look at our Web page!
http://www.chroniclebooks.com/spot7

It has no wings, but it can fly.
It's fittest when it's fat.
But if it's lost its breath,
it's flat.

sneak peek
**Spot 7
School**

First published in the United States in 2007 by Chronicle Books LLC.

English type design by Ingrid Marini.
Typeset in Super Grotesk.
Manufactured in China.
ISBN-10 0-8118-5722-0
ISBN-13 978-0-8118-5722-2

Library of Congress Cataloging-in-Publication Data available.

Distributed in Canada by Raincoast Books
9050 Shaughnessy Street, Vancouver, British Columbia V6P 6E5

10 9 8 7 6 5 4 3 2 1

Chronicle Books LLC
680 Second Street, San Francisco, California 94107

www.chroniclekids.com

SPot 7